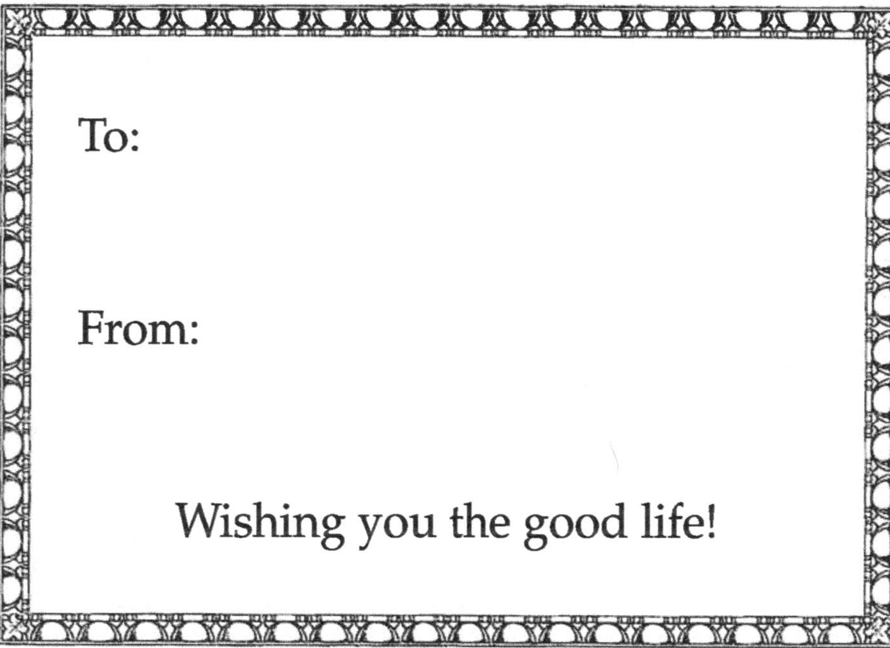

To:

From:

Wishing you the good life!

AF264746

KID SCRIPTS

Just What the Doctor Ordered

The Coloring Companion to *The Call of Life*

by Rudy Kachmann, M. D.

Illustrated by Dan Lynch

Rudy Kachmann M.D.

As a neurosurgeon of nearly forty years, Dr. Rudy Kachmann has witnessed firsthand, the devastating effects of risky and unhealthy behavioral practices on people's lives. This impressed upon him the need to encourage others to make conscious positive choices that will ultimately enhance the quality and length of their lives.

Mission Statement

To improve human behavior, families, and inter-personal relations through character development and the advancement of good health habits in an atmosphere of openness that will lead to better lives and building more peaceful communities.

ISBN: 13: 978-0692143537

Library of Congress Control Number: 2005908292

KID SCRIPTS

Twenty Prescriptions for Living the Good Life

Kid Scripts is the child centered coloring companion to *The Call of Life: Twenty Prescriptions for Living the Good Life* by Dr. Rudy Kachmann. Collectively, these twenty scripts create a plan for living our lives in caring, peaceful, and healthy ways. Because we are not born into this life with an instinctive inclination toward good character and virtuous living, these qualities must be modeled and taught to our young. It has become even more imperative and timely, given the world we live in today, to begin this process during the most formative years of our children's lives.

It is our hope, that each of the prescriptions in *Kid Scripts* will serve as discussion starters for children and their families; and by reflecting on the illustrations as they are colored, these good living choices will begin to take root in the hearts and minds of our youngest.

Kid Script One

Treat others as
you would like to be treated.

Kid Script Two

Be honest,
even when no one is looking.

Kid Script Three

Treat life with care;
avoid risky behavior.

Kid Script Four

Practice respect for authority;
parents, teachers, police
and government.

Kid Script Five

Be aware of physical
and mental abuse.

Kid Script Six

Read every day.

20 WAYS TO A GOOD LIFE
KID SCRIPTS

Kid Script Seven

Be tolerant
of others' beliefs.

Kid Script Eight

Express love, honor and respect
for your family.

Kid Script Nine

Become a life-long
learner.

Kid Script Ten

Show respect for all life,
human and animal.

Kid Script Eleven

Avoid violence;
become a peacemaker.

Kid Script Twelve

Celebrate the
differences in people.

Kid Script Thirteen

Strive to be your
best self.

Knowledge
WISDOM
Character

Kid Script Fourteen

Practice healthy living
in mind and body.

Kid Script Fifteen

Respect your body;
avoid tobacco, alcohol, and drugs.

Kid Script Sixteen

Help those who are
suffering or in need.

Kid Script Seventeen

Wait to give yourself
in marriage.

Kid Script Eighteen

Expect to make your
own way in life.

Kid Script Nineteen

Be forgiving of
yourself and others.

Kid Script Twenty

Respect the environment.

KID SCRIBBLES

KID SCRIBBLES

KID SCRXIBBLES

KID SCRIBBLES

Prescriptions for Living the Good Life

- Treat others as you would like to be treated.
- Be honest and truthful, do not steal — make your word your bond.
- Treat life with care; avoid risky behavior.
- Practice showing respect for authority; parents, teachers, police and government.
- Do not let physical or mental abuse go unnoticed.
- Read a book — regularly.
- Be tolerant of others' beliefs.
- Express honor, love and respect for your family.
- Make a commitment to continue education throughout your life.
- Show respect for all life, human and animal.
- Avoid violence; practice non-violence, support peace.
- Celebrate our differences: sex, race, background, appearance and disabilities.
- Seek knowledge, wisdom, good character and pursue excellence.
- Practice health-control; exercise your mind and body.
- Do not abuse your body — avoid tobacco, alcohol and drugs.
- Help those who are suffering or in need.
- Avoid sex until you're married.
- Expect to make your own way in life.
- Practice charity — be willing to forgive yourself and others.
- Respect the environment.

Dr. Rudy Kachmann has been a neurosurgeon in Fort Wayne, Indiana since 1969. Through his own life experience and years of caring for others, Dr. Kachmann has learned what behavioral qualities form the foundation for a healthy, happy, and productive life for people of all ages. His *Twenty Prescriptions for Living the Good Life* are further explored in his book *The Call of Life*.

Dan Lynch has been drawing cartoons for most of his life, largely on the editorial pages of the *Fort Wayne Journal Gazette, the Kansas City Star* and in newspapers across the country through national syndication. Other books illustrated by Lynch are *Those Cars of Auburn, Aw Shucks! Another Junior League Cookbook, There's Gold in Them Thar Ills,* and *Dirty Little Secrets: Cartoons and Essays from the Previous Millenium and Beyond.*

ISBN 9780692143537

Marnie & Rob
and the
CHRISTMAS PARCEL
Written by Elisia Ray
Illustrated by Aaron R.